Original title:
Midnight Snowfall Reveries

Copyright © 2024 Creative Arts Management OÜ
All rights reserved.

Author: Thomas Sinclair
ISBN HARDBACK: 978-9916-94-520-9
ISBN PAPERBACK: 978-9916-94-521-6

Snowflakes Dancing to Night's Song

In pajamas snug, I take a peek,
Outside the window, the snowflakes speak.
They tumble down in a silly flurry,
Dancing like clowns, oh what a hurry!

The snowman waits with a carrot nose,
His eyes are buttons, but who really knows?
I'll build him beefy, or maybe skinny,
Then he'll join in, looking quite spinny!

With snowball fights that ignite our cheer,
I duck and weave, then disappear.
A snowball bounces off my friend's bald spot,
Laughter erupts, we forget the cold plot!

Under streetlights, the snow glistens bright,
Creating a scene full of silly delight.
I'll have a snow dance till the break of dawn,
And hope that my socks stay dry—come on!

Enclosed in a Whispering White

Snowflakes tickle my nose,
Can't catch them, oh how it goes.
Sleds are flying down the hill,
Laughter echoes, what a thrill.

Puppies chasing their own tails,
In a race where nobody fails.
Snowman's hat is way too big,
He wobbles like a dancing pig.

Hibernation's Peaceful Palette

Bears are curled in cozy nests,
Snoring sounds resemble jest.
Do they dream of honey pots,
Or tripping over chilly tots?

Birds are peek-a-booing in trees,
Chirping out the silliest pleas.
Winter's chill can't steal their cheer,
They gossip 'bout the frosty deer.

Moon-Drenched Snow Dreams

Under a moon that glows so bright,
Snowmen wiggle in the night.
One slips down a slope so steep,
With a noise that wakes the sheep.

Stars twinkle like sneaky eyes,
Watching snowball fights arise.
Here comes a snowball, oh dear me!
Hit my brother, now I flee!

Catching Dreams in Winter's Web

Icicles hang like toothy grins,
As winter's trickery begins.
Snowflakes dance like dizzy sprites,
While we giggle through frosty nights.

Cocoa spills on fuzzy socks,
Making us look like silly flocks.
With a splash and a wink, we cheer,
Let's make snow angels, my dear!

Secrets Cradled by the Winter's Breath

In the quiet of the night,
Snowflakes dance with delight.
A snowman wearing a hat,
Whispers secrets to a cat.

Frosty critters run around,
Chasing dreams without a sound.
An old tree shakes its frosty brow,
"Who stole my branches? Not allowed!"

Veiled Night in a Shroud of White

Fluffy blankets cover all,
As I bounce, I nearly fall.
Snow angels flapping, oh so wide,
But the snowball fight's my pride.

Noses red, we laugh and play,
Chasing snowflakes on display.
I slip, I slide, straight down the hill,
At least my hot cocoa's a thrill!

Frozen Illusions Beneath the Stars

Snowmen grin with carrot noses,
But their laughter nothing poses.
A reindeer slips, then does a spin,
While all the snowflakes start to grin.

Fairy lights beckon all around,
With twinkling giggles, joy abound.
Sledding down a twisty track,
The hot dog cart bursts, who needs a snack?

Ethereal Light in the Frosted Air

Icicles dangle like old strings,
While winter teases with its flings.
A squirrel's stash, oh what a jest,
Did he just hide his nuts in my vest?

Pine trees shimmer in the glow,
While laughter echoes, to and fro.
Snowflakes fall with playful cheer,
And chase away our winter fear.

Hushed Mirth in the Icicles

A snowman wearing shades, so cool,
He dances like a goofball in the pool.
Fluffy flakes tickle, a giggling fight,
While penguins play poker under the moonlight.

Snowballs tossed by squirrels in glee,
A balmy winter, bizarre as can be.
With hot cocoa served in a frozen mug,
Even the snowflakes are ready to hug!

Frost-kissed Fantasies Unveiled

Santa's sleigh lost his GPS, oh dear,
Guided by reindeer who drank too much beer.
Elves tangled in lights, what a sight to see,
Frosty the snowman joined a jamboree!

Snowflakes giggle, swirling around,
While penguins waddle, looking profound.
A blizzard of laughter covers the town,
As icicles chuckle in outfits of crown.

Ethereal Silence in the Dark

The quiet whispers of snowflakes fall,
Chatty chipmunks having a ball.
Caught in a snowdrift, a cat starts to sneeze,
Its owner laughs, lips frozen with tease.

Night draped in white, moonbeams frolic,
While ice-skating on rooftops feels quite symbolic.
A snowball fight starts with a toss so sly,
And icicles shiver, "Oh my, oh my!"

Tread Softly on a Dreamscape

A fluffy rabbit hops with flair,
Dressed in a tux, he's quite debonair.
Snowflakes perform their dazzling tricks,
While waking up the sleeping wicks.

A carousel of snow, spinning around,
Each flake laughs, making whimsical sound.
Snowman's got tales to spin and weave,
In frozen realms, it's hard to believe!

The Enchantment of a Frozen Night

In a world of snowflakes, oh what a sight,
Even squirrels in hats dance with delight!
The moon made a sled, shining so bright,
While penguins in pajamas take off in flight.

A snowman who giggles, wearing a scarf,
Tells bad jokes that make the owls laugh hard.
The stars play a tune, strumming like guitars,
While rabbits do tango beneath the night stars.

Chasing Shadows on a Snowy Path

With snowballs a-flying, I'm dodging with glee,
Chasing my shadow like it's trying to flee.
My boots filled with snow—it's a slippery spree,
But the laughter we're sharing is wild and free.

Footprints keep flopping, what a curious dance,
While I slip and I slide, joining in the prance.
A snow angel whispers, 'Come join the romance,'
As I tumble and roll, lost in a chance.

Crystal Gems in the Stillness

Frosty reflections, like glittering beads,
The world's turned a canvas for hilarious deeds.
Icicles dangle as jesters, the leads,
While we tiptoe in laughter, forgetting our needs.

A snowflake named Freddy swirls in the air,
Complaining of frostbite, sings without care.
He giggles and flutters, 'I'm fine, don't you stare!'
It's a frosty cabaret, so lively and rare!

The Velvet Touch of Winter's Embrace

The chill wraps around us like a cozy surprise,
Where snowflakes are pillows, and snowmen wear ties.
They gossip like neighbors under starry skies,
As we toast marshmallows with giggles and sighs.

The air's filled with chuckles from snow-covered trees,
Who sway in the breeze like they're buzzing with bees.
In this frosty fairytale, one's worries just freeze,
While winter's sweet humor puts everyone at ease.

Enchanted Silence of the Evening

Under the glow of a streetlight,
A snowman dreams of a snow fight.
His carrot nose wears a frown,
As kids launch snowballs all around.

Squirrels in scarves prepare for the fray,
Chasing each other in a frosty ballet.
Giggles echo with every slip,
A fluffy white winter, a joyful trip.

The dog in a sweater, quite out of style,
Dances in joy and runs a few miles.
Snowflakes land on his nose with glee,
As he barks at shadows, wild and free.

An icicle hangs, a curious drip,
It wonders if it should take a dip.
The laughter rises with each little fight,
In this quirky world of pure white delight.

Wisp of Wonder in Every Flake

Each flake falls with a quirky twist,
They giggle as they land, can't resist.
Snowflakes whisper silly little tales,
Of snowmen who wear mismatched pails.

A choir of squirrels sings off-key,
Preparing for winter's jubilee.
They practice their moves on the snowy stage,
In this frosty wonderland, they engage.

The moon peers in, a curious sight,
It chuckles at shadows that dance at night.
With every gust of wind so sly,
The flakes spin and twirl, oh my, oh my!

In puffy coats and fuzzy hats,
Children throw snowballs at friendly cats.
The world can't help but smile and sway,
As laughter fills the frosty display.

Midwinter's Touch of Enchantment

Fluffy clouds toss white confetti,
As penguins waddle, feeling quite petty.
They slip and slide on the gleaming ice,
"Oh, who knew winter could be so nice?"

A bunny hops, sporting tiny boots,
Searching for carrots, oh, what a hoot!
Each thump on the ground makes a soft sound,
As he digs around, snow swirling around.

The trees wear coats, adorned and grand,
While whispering secrets, they all understand.
The laughter of winter dances in the air,
A chorus of joy, beyond compare.

Snowball fights break out, oh what a scene,
With giggles and cheers, always unforeseen.
A twirl, a tumble, and then the fun,
These winter nights shine like the sun!

A Tapestry of Snowy Allure

The porch light flickers, a winter star,
While snowflakes gather, near and far.
Underneath blankets, pets curl and snooze,
While children plot their next big moves.

The hot cocoa brews, marshmallows afloat,
A tiny penguin has stolen a coat.
With feathers displaced, he waddles with flair,
An adventurer bold in the chilly air.

A snow angel flops and laughs in delight,
Her wings a disaster, not quite right.
But in the stillness, her joy paints the night,
In the magical wonder, oh, what a sight!

As the snowflakes dance in the lunar glow,
Every moment sparkles with a whimsical flow.
The laughter and cheer fill the wintry expanse,
In a festive charade, we all join the dance.

Ink and Snowflakes Under Moonlight

Under the moon, a swirling dance,
Snowflakes twirl in a silly prance.
They land on noses, hats, and cheeks,
Making snowmen with frosty streaks.

A penguin slips on ice with flair,
Waddling past a startled bear.
Snowball fights among trees so tall,
Laughter echoes, a joyful call.

Frosty eyebrows, grins all around,
Icicles hung like jewels found.
Hot cocoa spills, a comical sight,
As snowflakes dance in pure delight.

Chasing shadows, we tumble and fall,
Snow angels made, we're having a ball.
With snowmen hats and carrot noses,
Winter's humor in joyful poses.

Tranquil Wishes in Silver

In silver light, we share our dreams,
While snowflakes giggle, it seems.
A cozy fire puts us at ease,
With snowmen posing like models, tease!

Twinkling lights on trees so bright,
A squirrel attempts an acorn flight.
Bouncing off snow, it makes a splash,
Landing right in a cold snow stash.

Whimsical wishes upon each flake,
While snowball warriors plan their break.
We giggle at the chaos we make,
In this chilly wonderland, none shall shake.

As dreams take flight on winter's wing,
We know the laughter this night will bring.
Frosty cheeks and a playful shove,
Together we revel, oh how we love!

Slumbering Landscapes of Light

The world is silent, wrapped in white,
While snowflakes prank in the soft moonlight.
They fall like whispers, a playful crowd,
Each landing softly, proud and loud.

A deer leaps high, a jump quite grand,
Slipping slightly in the frosty land.
Snowflakes tickle its twitching nose,
As laughter under starlight grows.

Our breath forms clouds, misty and white,
As we chase shadows, giggling, in fright.
A tumble here, a slip over there,
Creating a scene beyond compare.

With each flake, mischief is sown,
As snowmen chuckle, no reason to moan.
In a landscape of joy, we find our way,
Letting the fun lead our play.

The Night's Crystal Poetry

The night wears a gown of sparkling snow,
While figures frolic with a cheeky glow.
Snowflakes land like jokes on our heads,
Spinning tales as laughter spreads.

Chasing shadows with zigzag grace,
Falling snowball hits, a frosty embrace.
A cat darts by, escaping the clatter,
As snowflakes giggle and pitter-patter.

A warm mug tipped, what a silly sight,
Chocolaty mustaches, oh what delight!
The world now feels like a dream come true,
With snowflakes dancing, just me and you.

Together we'll build what makes us smile,
Crafting wonders with a little style.
In the nights wrapped snug in snowy fluff,
We find our joy, it's more than enough.

Serene Reflections of Winter's Charm

Snowflakes dance like clumsy ballet,
Falling down on a cat's tight sway.
The dog slips, makes a silly frown,
While birds laugh from their frosty crown.

Hot cocoa spills on winter's shirt,
Round the fire, my socks are dirt.
The snowman grins with a carrot nose,
But his hat's from last year's garden hose.

Chasing snowballs, what a sight,
Someone's face gets hit just right.
Giggling fits in the chilly air,
As penguin-people collapse in despair.

Sledding down a hill that's steep,
Turning into a snowy heap.
In dreams we fly, at least we try,
But here we are, just me and pie.

A Tapestry Woven with Snowflakes

Decembers weave a wintry thread,
With fabric soft as butter spread.
I tried to make a snow angel bright,
But looked more like a bird in flight.

Every snowball starts a fight,
With misshaped spheres that take to flight.
The neighbor's yard becomes our field,
Where rogue snowmen refuse to yield.

The paths we make are zig and zag,
Where visions turn into a lag.
And laughing fits freeze all sound,
As snowflakes spin and twirl around.

At night we build a fort so grand,
Using snow like a master's hand.
Yet just one slip, a tumble down,
Turns a king into a snowy clown.

Night's Breath on a Cold Meadow

Stars twinkle like eyes in the night,
While snow sings softly, pure delight.
A penguin slides past, looking cool,
His tuxedo stiff, a snowy fool.

Footprints stamp in a jolly trace,
Leading to cocoa at a slow pace.
Laughter echoes, fills the dark,
With snowflakes dancing, a winter lark.

Hares leap and bounce with flair,
While I trip over my own pair.
My scarf's tied in a comical knot,
Like a silly puzzle I forgot.

Under the glow of a moonlit beam,
We dream of hot tubs and whipped cream.
Yet here we are, shivering some,
In a frosty party, oh, what fun!

Undisturbed Slumber in the Snow

The world is wrapped in fluffy white,
While I snore loudly, what a fright!
The snowflakes tickle my nose oh so,
While my dreams dance in the frosty glow.

A squirrel sneaks up, oh what a tease,
He steals my sandwich, just with ease.
While I sleep on, what's this game?
Life's a circus, not quite tame.

The snowman winks with eyes of coal,
Making wishes for my school role.
But as I snore, the world's so still,
Silent giggles with snowy thrill.

Dreams of spring make me grin wide,
Yet here I lay, in fluff I bide.
Tomorrow's troubles seem so far,
While I snooze beneath this frosty star.

Celestial Silence on a Snowy Night

The flakes fell down like popcorn balls,
Tickling noses, as winter calls.
Sleds zoomed past, with giggles loud,
While snowmen strutted, oddly proud.

A cat in boots, so very spry,
Chasing shadows that twirl and fly.
With every leap, a puff of white,
Creating chaos in the night.

Kids in gear, all bundled tight,
Transform the street into pure delight.
Watch out for snowballs, dodge and weave,
Or you'll end up with your nose in eave!

From frozen noses to laughter's cheer,
We dance between the chilly sphere.
Under the moon with a twinkling spite,
Snow covers all with pure delight.

Moonlit Canvas of Softness

The sky above, a canvas bright,
Brushstrokes of snow paint the night.
A rabbit hops with fluffy pride,
Wearing snowflakes as a guide.

In this wonder, a cat takes aim,
Chasing snowflakes—it's no shame!
Slipping, sliding, up and down,
Who knew snow could make a clown?

Snowballs thrown with no regret,
Squealing laughter, not quite a threat.
A slide, a tumble, oh what fun!
Under the watch of the gleaming sun.

Whispers of winter, a cheeky tease,
While snowflakes fall like giggling bees.
In the chill, what warmth we find,
In jolly play, hearts intertwined.

Dreams Wrapped in Winter's Embrace

With twinkling stars and a chilled parade,
We race through snow like a grand charade.
A tumble, a fumble, off the track,
With snowflakes stuck upon our back.

A puppy leaps and turns around,
In snowdrifts deep—what fun we found!
Snowy beards on kids, oh so chic,
They melt away while we all speak.

In fluffy boots, we stomp and play,
As winter's chill turns night to day.
With giggles loud, we build our scene,
A kingdom made of silver sheen.

Slippery slopes make quite a sight,
As friendly ghosts of kids take flight.
In sparkling dreams of winter's cheer,
We laugh and dance, our hearts sincere.

Nightfall's Whisper in the Snow

A whispering snow, soft and grand,
Tickles the toes and fills the land.
Chubby cheeks and snowy grins,
Bouncing about in playful spins.

The hushed world plays hide-and-seek,
As snowflakes dance with a little squeak.
A snowman's hat flies off with glee,
While freezing fingers sneak a peek.

Two squirrels argue a fuzzy acorn,
As they wear hats made of shimm'ring horn.
With flair and spin, they join the show,
Amidst the sparkling, drifty glow.

The moon up high, a giggling host,
As frosty jests make us all toast.
So revel in mirth beneath the stars,
In swirling snow, we chase our cars!

Whirling Dreams in Winter's Grip

Spinning like a top, I twirl,
Chasing snowflakes in a whirl.
My nose is cold, my toes do freeze,
Yet here I dance with perfect ease.

A snowman grins, with button eyes,
Wearing my hat; oh, what a surprise!
He tumbles down with laughter loud,
As I trip over, feeling proud.

In drifting drifts, I lose my shoe,
While squirrels mock, they laugh and coo.
Fluffy friends of winter's play,
Join me in this grand ballet.

Through frosty dreams, we fly and glide,
On ice-bound paths, we slip and slide.
With giggles shared in chilly air,
Who knew snow could bring such flair?

Nocturnal Garden of Snow Daisies

In a garden made of dream,
Snow daisies peek with frosty gleam.
A cat in boots prances around,
Meowing poems, not making a sound.

The moon is bright, the stars are sassy,
They whisper secrets like they're classy.
I sprinkle snowflakes on my nose,
And dance with shadows from my toes.

A rabbit hops in a fancy hat,
Sipping cocoa, but where's the cat?
He's lost in tales of snowy lore,
Thank goodness there's room for more!

We giggle through this chilly spree,
In a land where winter's wild and free.
With each snow petal that lands with grace,
We find our laughter's favorite place.

Frosted Lullabies in Twilight

Under blankets piled up high,
I hear a whisper, a jovial sigh.
Hot cocoa spills as the snowflakes fall,
My teddy snickers, the room's a brawl.

The clock strikes twelve, but who really cares?
I'm convinced that penguins can climb stairs.
As snowmen throw snowballs with zest,
I snuggle deeper, who needs rest?

In dreams, I travel to lands of cream,
Where marshmallow clouds make everything a dream.
With chocolate rivers and candy trees,
I float on snowflakes with perfect ease.

The lullabies play soft and sweet,
While giggles wrap me like tasty treats.
In this frosted world where joy takes flight,
I dance with dreams through the starry night.

The Hush After the Storm

After the ruckus, silence reigns,
Snow blankets chaos, beauty gains.
A squirrel sits, looking quite bemused,
He's wearing a hat that's brightly fused.

Icicles hang like glittering shards,
While snowballs form for friendly guards.
A snow angel waves, how cute is that?
But oh dear, here comes a flying cat!

The world is hushed, but not for long,
Children giggle, singing a song.
Snow shovels clash with joyful pow,
As snowflakes dance and laugh somehow.

With warmth in hearts, we play and cheer,
Frosty fun brings all near.
In this tranquil, snowy retreat,
Life's a joke, and oh, so sweet!

Poetry Written in the Frost

My fingers wrote a line so neat,
On frosted glass, where friends do meet.
But then the cat came with a paw,
And turned my sonnet into a flaw.

I blame the snowflakes for their dance,
They left me stuck in a silly trance.
They giggle as they tumble down,
And cover up my frosty frown.

I thought I'd craft a winter tale,
Instead, I slipped and lost my trail.
The snowmen laugh, they think it's grand,
As I flail about, without a plan.

So here's my ode, both silly and bright,
To frosty nights and laughter's light.
The snow may chill, but hearts are warm,
In the chaos, joy takes form.

The Twilight Freeze of Dreams

When winter whispers with a chill,
I grab my hat with goofy thrill.
But all the snowflakes know my name,
As they drift by, just playing games.

I built a snowman, gave it flair,
With mismatched socks and crazy hair.
But as I turned to grab a drink,
That snowman wobbled, made me think.

They say the cold can freeze your gait,
I slipped and landed—what a fate!
The dog just laughed, he passed me by,
While I lay there beneath the sky.

With dreams of snowball fights so grand,
I lost the battle, slipped on land.
Yet joy remains, though bruised, it's true,
In snowy nights, we start anew.

Flakes of Joy in Glistening Light

Oh, how the flakes fall, soft and round,
Like fluffy marshmallows on the ground.
But watch your step, it's quite a scene,
For unexpected slides, you may not glean.

Hot cocoa spills as I sip and stare,
The snowmen dance like they don't care.
While squirrels scurry with tiny treats,
And winter's echo drums up the beats.

I tried to catch a flake on my tongue,
Instead it landed where it's hung.
My face turned bright red, a true delight,
As I laughed at the soft, silly sight.

So here's to laughter 'neath winter skies,
Where joy and snowflakes come as a prize.
In every slip and frosty cheer,
There's magic in every snowy sphere.

Winter's Lullaby of Purest White

As night descends, the world wears white,
A canvas fresh, a perfect sight.
But oh, the twists that nature bends,
As winter plays with me and friends.

The trees wear hats of powdered fluff,
And even snowmen look quite tough.
Yet when they melt, they leave behind,
A puddle that's not so well-defined.

My boots are stuck, I'm half a goat,
The laughter echoes, I'll stay afloat!
Through icy paths and frosty trees,
I giggle through each winter sneeze.

So gather round and play the game,
In sparkling snow, we're all the same.
With every fall and merry cheer,
The warmth of joy brings winter near.

Frosty Haze and Shadow Games

Lapdogs in parkas, prancing with flair,
Chasing their tails as they dance in the air.
Snowmen wobble, their noses askew,
While kids giggle loud, shouting, "You too!"

Whispers of snowflakes, like tickles in flight,
Frosty the jester, he giggles at night.
Yet squirrels in boots, looking stylish and bold,
Share secrets with rabbits; the stories unfold.

Fluffy white hats on each frosty friend,
Creating a kingdom where laughter won't end.
Hot cocoa spills on a snow-covered scene,
As marshmallows salute both the silly and serene.

Hats flap and flap in the crumbs of a breeze,
While snowflakes float down with effortless ease.
The moon winks at mischief, it knows all the jokes,
It's a chilly wild party where everyone pokes.

Dance of the Winter Spirits

Bouncing like popcorn, the flakes come alive,
They twirl and they spin, it's a snowflake jive.
Goblins in mittens are mixing a brew,
While elves play hopscotch with the frosty crew.

Whiskers of frost on a cat's little nose,
As penguins moonwalk, the chaos just grows.
Laughter wraps round like a warm woollen scarf,
While frostbitten gnomes share their best winter laugh.

The stars giggle softly as shadows parade,
A snowball fight breaks out; oh, the plans that we've made!
Snow forts emerging, a fortress of cheer,
With tiptoeing critters in the frosty veneer.

Top hats and mittens, so plaid and so bright,
Outrageous fashion, a late winter night.
Impromptu ballet of the icy and brave,
Dancing through snowfall, oh, we misbehave!

Stillness Gripped in a White Cloak

In the quiet of night, under blankets we ease,
A snowman's got fashion, with cozy, warm fleece.
While whispers of warmth curl up in the air,
The cocoa's too hot for a snowman to share.

Pajamas of flannel, warm slippers in place,
While ghosts of hot chocolate start racing in space.
Silly snowflakes tumble, a flurry of fun,
While the sun's just a rumor; they say it has run.

Pine trees are giggling, their branches all swayed,
While shadows in boots get a wild escapade.
A snow angel flops in the fluff with delight,
As laughter ignites the crispness of night.

Blanketed dreams in a whimsical game,
Each shimmer of frost, a tickle or flame.
But just like a snowman, we melt in a breeze,
This stillness won't last; let's laugh, if you pleese!

Sweet Surrender to Frosted Dreams

Winter's not grumpy; he's just feeling bold,
As kittens in boots stroll outside in the cold.
With each step they take, giggles scatter like seeds,
And frost-covered flowers fulfill winter's needs.

Trees wear their snow like a fluffy white coat,
While snowflakes conspire, plotting each little note.
A ballet of breezes makes mischief tonight,
But the laughter of kids is the true winter light.

Sugarplums dance in a hooded delight,
While snowmen keep secrets, hidden from sight.
Sledding down hills, they tumble and glide,
Each roll and each roll is a joyride outside.

Soft whispers of frost wrap the world like a hug,
And dreams take to flight as we wiggle and shrug.
So gather your friends, let's spin through the chill,
For fun never melts when there's laughter to spill.

Frosted Symphony of Silence

In the night, the flakes prepare,
To blanket rooftops everywhere.
The squirrels slip, a sight to see,
Creating chaos with glee.

A snowman waddles, nose of a carrot,
A top hat borrowed from the parrot.
His arms are twigs, all akimbo,
He looks ridiculous, oh my, oh no!

The snowflakes giggle, fluttered and spun,
As kids tumble down, oh what fun!
Pompoms on mittens, mismatched and bright,
Crafting snowballs with all their might.

Whispers of snowmen, secrets abound,
While the birds chirp, hopping around.
The trees wear white, a fashionable cloak,
Even the moon bursts out a joke!

Celestial Dances in White

Underneath the twinkling stars,
Snowflakes waltz in joyful spars.
The puppies leap, their tails a blur,
With snowballs flying, what a stir!

A snow angel flops with blissful grace,
Spreading wings in a frosty embrace.
Then up he gets, a frosty grin,
Only to land in a heap again!

The shadows chuckle as snowmen tease,
Sleds are racing with utmost ease.
A mitten drops, a toe is cold,
While laughter echoes, a joy untold.

Chasing their hats through winter's laugh,
Snow drifts pile like mischief's craft.
A flurry of fun, as giggles abound,
In the quiet night, joy is found!

Echoes of Snow-laden Dreams

Dreams tumble down like snow on the ground,
With giggles and shouts, we all gather 'round.
A snow fort built, as tall as can be,
Who knew ice and snow could be so free?

The raccoon rolls in, snatching a snack,
Waddles away with a nut from the pack.
Snowflakes spin, like they've had too much,
Dancing madly, oh what a touch!

In winter's embrace, the kittens prance,
With paws in the snow, in a funny dance.
The wonders of winter, a playful art,
Turning chilly nights into merry heart!

Socks on the cat, a hilarious sight,
As he leaps and pounces, full of delight.
In a world wrapped in frosty delight,
Laughter erupts, oh what a night!

Twilight's Embrace of Frost

In twilight's hold, snowflakes start,
Twinkling like diamonds in a clandestine art.
A penguin slips, but tries to stride,
Oh, what a dance down the snowy slide!

The snow clumps together, eager to play,
As children yell, 'Snowball fight, hurray!'
But who will win when mittens are thrown,
A battle of giggles, nobody's alone!

Chasing the flakes that swirl like a dream,
All bundled up, they plot and they scheme.
One falls flat, dressed like a snow-king,
While making a snowman, they find daffodils sing!

Snowflakes giggle, as they pile high,
A whirlwind of silliness in the sky.
With every drift, laughter ignites,
In this frosty world, pure delight bites!

Reverie in the Winter Glow

A penguin slipped right on its toes,
The snowman chuckled, then froze.
Sleds spun 'round like a wild dance,
As snowflakes giggled in a trance.

Snowballs flew in a frosty fight,
One hit a cat, what a sight!
The dog dove in with joy on high,
Leaving a trail as he flew by.

The hot cocoa spilled with glee,
As snowflakes whispered, "Come play with me!"
A snow angel flopped with a grand flair,
Then got up laughing without a care.

Under twinkling stars, we sing,
Joining the frost, what joy it brings!
Let's laugh and dance till we can't stand,
As winter pets us with a gentle hand.

Secrets Drift on the Snowy Air

Whispers float on frozen winds,
A squirrel chats and grins with friends.
Snowflakes swirl like little spies,
They hold secrets and snowy lies.

A rabbit hops with a twist and turn,
Sinks in white, oh how we yearn!
The chicken waddles with a proud flair,
While snow drifts rest on its fluffy hair.

Frosty whispers, a giggle shared,
As snowflakes tangle in curls unprepared.
A bear in a cap takes a stroll,
With snowflakes bouncing like a lively troll.

In the crisp night, laughter rings,
As winter's prankster softly sings.
Let's gather 'round, old tales retell,
In this snowy, fun-filled carousel.

Holding Dreams in a Snow Flurry

A hat flew off, and what a spree!
The wind stole it, oh not from me!
A snowman further laps up frost,
  While searching for a carrot lost.

Snowflakes tickle, little feet dance,
  Is this a winter wonder chance?
A penguin slides and takes a fall,
While ducks marvel, having a ball.

Frosty chortles, "Can you believe?
Silly snow from a frozen weave!"
Time for cocoa, warm by the fire,
  But first, a snowball to inspire.

Under night skies, laughter flows,
Wrapped in the warmth, time just glows.
With dreams tossed like snow, oh so bright,
  Tomorrow awaits in pure delight.

Nighttime Reveries on Soft Snow

In the hush, a snowman dreams,
While snowflakes giggle in moonbeams.
A cat with boots jumps up for cheer,
Only to land with a snowy smear.

Mice in scarves dart the lane,
Wearing hats in this playful domain.
Each tumble brings a chorus, a cheer,
As winter's whimsy draws us near.

Rabbits race with a thumping heart,
Sliding in snow, what a fun art!
A snowball fight blossomed wide,
While squirrels watch, cheeks puffed with pride.

Frozen giggles fill the air,
With frosty marbles here and there.
In this winter flush, we all play,
Chasing snowflakes till break of day.

Dreamscapes in Icy Reflections

I dreamt I was a snowflake, light,
Dancing in the moon's soft sight.
But I tripped on a coldling's hat,
And landed on a plump cat.

The cat just stared, eyes wide as bowls,
While I whispered, 'Don't eat my souls!'
I wiggled and jiggled with mayhem flair,
As the kitty plotted my fluffy affair.

In clouds of white, we strayed and spun,
Finding snowmen made of ginger buns.
They waved with hands crafted from pie,
As I thought, 'Oh dear, why did I fly?'

Then with a frosty tickle, I was gone,
The cat purred softly, 'Back to my lawn.'
So here I am, a tale biennial,
Don't tell my friends about the feline, venial.

Flurries of Hope in the Night

Across the ground, a quilt of white,
Snowflakes twirled in wild delight.
I built a snowman, stout and round,
With peanut butter cups I found.

He blinked at me with a cookie frown,
'Where'd you find such a big ol' crown?'
I chuckled back and donned a grin,
'You're the king of all, let the fun begin!'

Snowball fights erupted, oh so grand,
Until one hit me, I dropped my stand.
I tumbled across the icy gleam,
Rolling like a frosted dream.

But laughter echoed through the trees,
As snow fell softly, with the breeze.
So here we jest, each flake a cheer,
In this frozen world, let's stay right here.

The Calm Before the Winter's Call

The world's asleep, all wrapped in white,
Not a creature stirring this silent night.
A rabbit hopped, slipped on its ear,
And danced the tango, oh dear, oh dear!

I made a snow angel, winged and proud,
When suddenly, I drew a crowd.
The squirrel said, 'That's not quite right,'
And fluffed my halo with a shout of spite!

With laughter shared, time drifted slow,
As marshmallow meteors fell from the snow.
Hot cocoa brewed, my cup did fizz,
I sipped with glee while giggling his.

So here's to moments, quirky and bright,
Before the winter takes its flight.
In these cold hours, let's be our best,
And revel in the laughter, our cozy fest!

Frostbitten Fantasies of the Mind

In a world of flakes, peculiar sight,
Gnomes played tag under the pale moonlight.
One slipped, fell flat upon his bum,
I laughed so hard, nearly bit my gum.

With frosty breath, my thoughts took flight,
Dreaming of a penguin in a snazzy suit, alright!
He waddled by with a mug of tea,
'What's good, my friend? Let's sip with glee!'

The whimsy danced in a snowball's flight,
While frost-tipped trees glittered with delight.
A snowshoe hare hosted a grand parade,
With sunshine smiles, our worries fade.

As dawn approached, we waved goodbye,
To dreams of snowflakes that wave so high.
With laughter ringing, my heart felt light,
And I embraced the chill of the night.

Whispers of the Silent Drift

In pajamas warm, I stumble out,
To greet the snow without a doubt.
I slip and slide, a frosty dance,
As snowflakes giggle, oh what a chance!

The world is blank, like my old fridge,
But my face I make, a little smidge.
With snowballs packed, I lob with glee,
Then fall flat on my back, oh me! oh me!

The trees wear coats, all fluffy and white,
While I create a snowman's delight.
He grins at me, with buttons and charm,
One eye's a button, the other— a farm!

Yet as I laugh in winter's embrace,
I spot a snow hare, what a funny face!
He hops away, with a flick of his tail,
I ponder his antics over a warm ale!

Frosted Dreams on the Windowpane

Outside my window, a world all aglow,
With frosted patterns where reindeer might go.
I swear I saw Santa, in flip-flops and shorts,
While snowflakes flip documents in funny reports!

I take a sip of cocoa, all marshmallow tops,
And watch as the snow makes my garden look tops.
The cat pounces out, he's bonkers tonight,
With snow on his nose, oh, what a silly sight!

Each flake's a whisper of laughter and fun,
As I take on the task to create a new run.
But down I go in a belly flop spree,
I laugh as I ponder, that snow's winning me!

Now I'll build a castle, or so I may boast,
A kingdom of laughter, my fluffy snow host.
With turrets of ice, and a door made of cheer,
I'll reign as the queen, let's bring on the beer!

Lullabies of the Winter Veil

Cracks sound beneath my wandering feet,
Like old grandpa's back, a funny repeat.
With twinkles and giggles, the stars pull me near,
While I trip over snow, not a hint of fear!

My hot cocoa spills, oh what a delight!
As I chase a snowflake, it takes off in flight.
It eludes my grasp, with a wink like a tease,
I carve out a snow angel, or just a big sneeze!

Frosty the snowman keeps rolling on by,
He stops when I point, and looks up to the sky.
"Do you hear that?" I ask, feeling quite bold,
"It's laughter and joy, breaking winter's cold!"

So I dance with the snow, in a curious swirl,
These silly little dreams make my heart twirl.
And under the glow of a lamp post so bright,
I'll laugh 'til I drop, oh what a true sight!

Starlit Echoes in the Chill

Starlight glimmers, the night feels so cool,
While I twirl with the snowflakes, oh what a fool!
They mimic my moves, such a charming parade,
As I try to keep up, but alas, I cascade!

The trees softly crackle, they chuckle away,
At my awkward dance in the soft moonlight play.
A snowball flies by, I dodge with a grin,
But it lands on my head, oh where have I been?

Sledding down hills, I catch my own breath,
While racing with rabbits, oh what fun bequeath!
I tumble and fumble, end up in a heap,
While snowmen gather 'round, in laughter deep!

So here's to the chill and the giggles it brings,
With snow on my nose and laughter that clings.
I'll dance 'til I'm dizzy, as spirits take flight,
In a world filled with whimsy, oh what a delight!

A Serenade of Snowy Reflections

The flakes dance down like clumsy fools,
With every twirl, they break the rules.
A snowman trips on his hat so tall,
His carrot nose is bound to fall.

The streetlights glow like eager eyes,
Witnessing all the frosty lies.
The winter air is crisp and neat,
But my tongue's frozen to my seat!

We gather round with cocoa mugs,
Sharing laughs and playful shrugs.
With snowball fights as loud as thunder,
Caught in snow, our joy, we wonder.

So let us cheer in winter's chill,
Laughing loud and dance at will.
For in this white and crazy night,
We'll fumble through till morning light.

The Night's Bouquet of Flurries

Snowflakes twirl like giggling sprites,
They land on noses, oh what sights!
Children tumble, falling down,
While frozen laughter fills the town.

The moon casts shadows, funny shapes,
On clumsy sleds, we make escapes.
A snowball whizzes past my ear,
And I just hope it's not too near!

Dogs leap high in cotton coats,
Chasing tails like playful boats.
They burrow deep in heaps of white,
And sneeze out snowballs with delight!

Through drifts we wade, it's quite a sight,
As snowflakes tumble, soft and light.
With giggles echoing through the night,
We celebrate this frosty flight.

Between The Stars and Frozen Fields

Amidst the stars, we make our tracks,
With crunching snow beneath our backs.
Frosty breath creates a cloud,
We giggle loudly, feeling proud.

The blanket white wraps 'round the trees,
Where squirrels hide from chilly breeze.
They peer at us with bulging eyes,
As we concoct our crazy lies.

A snowman wears my old brown hat,
And stands there looking quite a brat.
His buttons wink with sly intent,
As if he knows the joy we spent.

Oh winter night, with mischief near,
You bring us warmth, you bring us cheer.
We'll dance beneath the icy sky,
And laugh till morning draws nigh.

Muses of a Chilled Embrace

Frosty whispers weave their dreams,
While laughter bursts at snowball schemes.
We tumble down with gleeful yells,
In chilly winds, our story swells.

Glistening flakes like fairy dust,
We scatter hope, this night we trust.
A penguin waddles, bold and spry,
His icy antics make us cry.

With cheeks aglow and spirits high,
Our giggles chase the frosty sky.
A ballet dance on slopes of white,
What a funny, blissful flight!

So bundle up and take a chance,
In winter's grip, let's laugh and dance.
For in this world of crisp delight,
We find our joy, and everything's right.

Celestial Whispers Beneath the Snow

Under blankets, we all snore,
But the snow's a noisy door.
Chattering flakes, they laugh and tease,
Whispering secrets on the breeze.

Sleds soup up, with giggles galore,
Gliding down, we yearn for more.
Hot cocoa spills on the frosty ground,
Swirling like laughter all around.

The snowmen wear hats, askew and bright,
Eyes of buttons, such a sight!
They gossip about the kids nearby,
While snowballs form for ninja fights.

In the drifts, we stumble and fall,
Flailing arms, it's a grand brawl.
Yet in the chaos, joy takes flight,
Dancing beneath the soft moonlight.

The Snow's Soft Embrace on Dreams

As the snowflakes fall, we declare,
Our pajamas the best, with pockets to spare.
Dreams of snowball fights galore,
While we sneak snacks from behind the door.

In the morning, a blanket of white,
Hide-and-seek in the frosty delight.
The cat trips over, a feline-induced spill,
Pawing at snowflakes with magical thrill.

Wiggly sleds race down the hill,
Cheering as frostbite we thrill;
We hurl our laughter like snowballs too,
Peaceful giggles, as the snowflakes flew.

Waltzing snowmen, you silly fools,
Making a ruckus, breaking our rules.
Yet beneath their silly and frosty craze,
We revel in joy, in wintry haze.

Luminary Nightfall in Frost

The stars above twinkle and blink,
While we sip cocoa, savoring the drink.
Whimsy dances in the frosty night,
As snowflakes swirl in playful flight.

With glowing lights on every tree,
The snow whispers jokes of glee.
While the snowmen can't keep their hats,
Chasing squirrels, they stage combat!

Our snow boots squeak like a silly tune,
Laughter echoes under the moon.
Huddles of friends make snow angels and shout,
"Look, I'm a bird! How do I get out?"

In the stillness, a snowball surprise,
Flying toward unsuspecting eyes.
With laughter ringing in frosty air,
We build our dreams, with no time to spare.

Veiled In the Silence of Flakes

In whispers soft, the snowflakes play,
Tickling our noses in a frosty ballet.
Hidden mischief in the still of night,
As dreams dance under the starlit light.

Snowflakes boogie while we snooze,
Making tiny snowmen in our shoes.
With mittens stuck and buttons askew,
We wake up to a surprise—who knew?

Around us, laughter like snowflakes flies,
While we dodge snowballs with wide-open eyes.
The dogs prance and leap with delight,
As winter's magic ignites our night.

In snowdrifts, we tumble, a sight to behold,
Wrapping up warmth in our scarves of gold.
With each fall, we greet the chilly ground,
In a play of snow, joy knows no bound.

Silver Shadows Beneath the Moon

Under the glow of a round cheese slice,
I sneezed on a snowman, oh what a price!
He toppled and giggled, a frosty surprise,
As snowflakes danced like tiny spies.

A rabbit in pajamas, he jumped in delight,
Wore fuzzy slippers, what a silly sight!
He offered me cocoa, said it's outta sight,
But it was just ice with air, oh what a fright!

The trees played charades, their branches would sway,
While squirrels in tuxedos joined in on the play.
They juggled acorns, oh what a display,
As I laughed so hard, I forgot the way!

With snowballs as grenades, we fought like the pros,
Until our noses brightened, like Rudolph's bold nose.
The moon winked at us, and our laughter just rose,
In this wintry wonderland, anything goes!

Crystal Serenades of the Night

A penguin in slippers just waddled right by,
With a top hat and cane, he hoped to fly high.
They say he's a magician, oh my oh my!
But when he tripped over, he wished he could cry.

A snowman was singing a goofy old song,
His carrot nose twitched, he was never quite wrong.
With a voice like a trumpet, it couldn't belong,
But he boogied along, it just felt so strong!

The stars glittered down like little confetti,
As flurries of snow made us feel all so jetty.
We danced in circles, oh wasn't it petty?
Hoping the cold would leave us all sweaty!

A reindeer was juggling, oh look at him go,
With candy canes flying, the wind put on a show.
We laughed till we cried, in the joy's warm glow,
In this crystal serenade, our hearts stole the show!

Enchanted Slumber in the Cold

As I lay on the ground, feeling fluffy and round,
A squirrel debated, should he leap or stick 'round?
In a hat two sizes too big, he looked quite profound,
Talking to snowflakes, without making a sound.

An owl with a monocle gave me a stage wink,
He thought he was cool with his fancy drink.
But in the brisk chill, we both paused to think;
Should we join the party, or head back and sink?

While bunnies made snow angels, their tails all a-fluff,
One tripped and fell, claiming it wasn't that tough.
We giggled and snickered, the night was quite rough,
But under the stars, we couldn't get enough!

In an enchanted slumber, the laughs felt so bright,
With friendships forged tightly under shimmering light.
So here's to the chill, and the winter's delight,
For every fluffy moment is truly just right!

Nocturnal Hush of Snowflakes

In a blanket of hush, the world took a pause,
As penguins performed with their best dance cause.
They slid on their bellies, with no need for applause,
Just hoping for warmth beneath winter's claw.

A candlelit snowball rolled under my feet,
But it turned into snowman, now isn't that sweet?
He chuckled and danced, said, 'You've got the beat!'
In the hush of the night, it turned quick to heat.

The breeze told the tales of the shenanigans near,
A cat with a scarf claimed he'd conquered the fear.
But stumbled and tumbled, with meows that were clear,
As laughter erupted, filled the chilly air!

In this hush of the night, the world came alive,
With snowflakes engaging in a frosty jive.
So let's fill our cups and get ready to thrive,
'Cause in this funny realm, how happy we strive!

Twilight Glimmers on Blankets White

The snowflakes twirl, a ballet so sweet,
Waltzing together, they tumble and meet.
A snowman grins with a carrot for a nose,
But where did he hide all his winter clothes?

With every flake that lands on my hat,
I can't help but wonder, where's my old cat?
She leaps through the drifts with a bound and a roll,
Then plops down to nap—oh, the queen of the hole!

The trees wear coats, all frosty and bright,
But my dog thinks the snow is a pure, tasty bite.
He snorts and he sneezes, then digs, oh the mess!
What joy does he find in this white wilderness?

But tonight, as we laugh by the warm, glowing fire,
I cherish each giggle that lifts me up higher.
Snowball fights burst, oh, what a wild fling!
Wrapped in cheer, winter's a most jolly thing.

Celestial Dances in Frosted Air

Stars sprinkle down like powdered sugar's grace,
As snowflakes dance in a whimsical race.
The moon, quite a joker, peeks through the trees,
Whispering secrets to the soft winter breeze.

A penguin in pajamas slides down from the peak,
Wobbling and wobbling—oh, isn't he sleek?
Skiing on belly, he zooms with great flair,
While snowmen are chuckling, they haven't a care.

Frosty hues shimmer on branches and streets,
While rabbits bounce by, oh what lively feats!
They hop on the snow, looking quite like a show,
As snowflakes applaud in their soft, swirly flow.

But winter is tricky, with pranks up its sleeve,
A slip on the ice—oh, you wouldn't believe!
We tumble, we giggle, then rise with a cheer,
Embracing the madness, we welcome the year.

Frosted Fantasies Under a Dark Sky

The world dressed in white looks fancy and neat,
While I struggle to find my warm, furry seat.
Snowballs go flying from each chilly hand,
As laughter erupts, it's a loud winter band.

The squirrels have gathered with nuts to exchange,
Debating which winter snacks they rearrange.
A blizzard of acorns falls with a crash,
While the birds sing a chorus under winter's bash.

The sleigh rides are crazy, with laughter galore,
As we race through the drifts, and then bump the floor.
Oh look at that goose, he's formed quite a crew,
A parade of odd friends, who knew they all flew?

Even shadows are dancing in frosty delight,
As we throw snowballs at each other, what a sight!
With giggles and joy, we'll cherish tonight,
And sing songs of snow under stars shining bright.

Ghosts of Winter's Gentle Touch

In winter's embrace, the chill hugs us tight,
As snowmen confess that they cannot take flight.
With eyes made of coal and a grin wide as cheese,
They ponder their fate in a world built on freeze.

The owls up above share their wisdom so sly,
As mittens unmatch in a chilly nearby.
They hoot and they laugh, a ruckus profound,
While snowflakes cascade, swirling all 'round.

Pine trees wear snow like a trendy new hat,
While visions of gingerbread dance, how about that?
The icicles glimmer, stealing the show,
Making playful jingles with wind's gentle blow.

We sip on hot cocoa while dreams take a spin,
Recalling the tales of the quirky and thin.
As winter's sweet ghosts flutter softly in white,
We bid them goodnight, under blankets of light.

Chasing Stardust in the Chill

A flake flew by, I tried to catch,
It landed softly, right on my hat.
I spin around, my arms out wide,
But now I'm stuck, oh what a ride!

The snowman grins, his nose a stick,
I swear he winked, oh that was slick.
I danced with joy, slipped on my face,
And now I'm part of this snowy race!

The cold laughs loud, my cheeks turn red,
Frosty friends tease, 'Get out of bed!'
We build a fort, let snowballs fly,
And I pretend to be that guy.

With frosty breath, we form a crowd,
I shout my dreams, oh so loud!
But in a flurry, I take a spree,
And bury my pals with glee, whee!

Luminescent Clouds Above

The stars are giggling, watch them twirl,
As fluffy clouds begin to swirl.
The moon yells, 'Hey, I want to play!'
A snowy party leads the way.

The light dances off the icy ground,
As I slip and glide, a silly sound.
I prance around, a whimsy sprite,
While snowflakes twinkle in the night.

A rabbit hops, he trips and falls,
We both burst out in laughter's calls.
With frozen toes that fidget and wiggle,
The frosty fun makes us jiggle!

We dance on air, with joy unfurled,\nAs winter's magic spins the world.
In a flurry of bliss, our laughter swells,
Underneath a sky where the whimsy dwells!

Serene Slumber Beneath the Flakes

Within white blankets, a dream takes hold,
A snowball fight? Oh, I'm feeling bold!
I snooze away amidst the fluff,
Yet secretly, I can't get enough.

A pillow fight breaks, as friends invade,
In this wintry world, we've got it made.
Flakes drift down, like giggles of cheer,
Making cozy wishes to keep us near.

Outside my window, the chill winds tease,
A shiver of fun, a flavorful breeze.
My sleepy head spins with tales untold,
While laughter lingers in the cold.

Dreams arise as the night does soar,
And smirks and chuckles define our lore.
With flurries of joy, we drift asleep,
Wrapped in frosty hugs, our hearts to keep!

Elysium in the Night Light

In a sparkling glow, the antics roll,
Snowmen wobble, and hearts are whole.
Under twinkling lights, we lose our fears,
With laughter that echoes through the years.

A snowball flies, it finds its mark,
On my friend's head, they give a spark!
With giggles bouncing, we run and hide,
Chasing happiness with snowflakes as our guide.

The silence breaks with voices bright,
As we weave through wonders in the night.
Rolling down hills, oh what a sight,
Drenched in glimmers, full of delight.

Frosty delights in a magical sphere,
The joy that lingers, forever near.
In this winter wonder, we dance with glee,
Seizing the laughter, wild and free!

Frozen Notes in the Quiet Gloom

In the chill of the night, I dance with my cat,
He twirls on the floor, and I laugh at that.
Snowflakes are falling, with great little flair,
We tiptoe on ice, like we just don't care.

The trees wear white coats, looking quite chic,
I tried to impress them, but all I could squeak.
They frown at my moves, frozen in place,
I'm a sight to behold, a snowman disgrace!

Hot cocoa in hand, I sip and I dream,
Of snowmen who gossip, or so it would seem.
With snowball debates on the latest gossip,
Is it winter that's silly, or just us who flip?

As the night grows deep, I giggle and squeal,
The snow makes me tumble, oh how I feel!
Tomorrow I'll build, maybe a bear,
But for now, I'll just nap on this frosty chair.

Silvery Twinkles on a Blank Page.

Oh look, it's a wonder, the snowflakes are bright,
They blink like they're winking at me in the night.
I scribble my dreams in the frosty old air,
As the squirrels in the trees give me a blank stare.

With a twist of my tongue, I taste the cold breeze,
It tickles my nose and makes me sneeze!
Dancing with shadows, I prance in delight,
While the stars roll their eyes at my silly plight.

The moon whispers secrets to fluff on the ground,
As I write down my thoughts that spin all around.
Like snowflakes, they drift, through the winks and the nods,
Round and round, just like my thoughts of the odds!

I'll make a snow angel, and then I'll take flight,
Wishing on twinkles that blink in the night.
For every soft landing is a giggle and glee,
Even the frost seems to chuckle with me!

Whispers of Winter's Veil

Amidst the soft hush, there's a tinkling sound,
Is it giggles or whispers that dance all around?
The snowflakes are giddy, they tumble and flip,
While I trip on my boots, oh what a slip!

The moon makes a face, a big round surprise,
With twinkling laughter that lights up the skies.
I waddle like penguins, my feet all askew,
As the snow gently covers my funny debut.

With snowmen conspiring, and scarf fashion jokes,
They chuckle and nod, those quirky old folks.
I swear there's a snowball that's scheming tonight,
It's plotting to sneak a soft hit in my sight!

So here in the twilight, surrounded by glee,
I toast to the snow and the stories we see.
With whimsy and laughter in layers so fine,
Winter's chill tickles, oh how it's divine!

Dreams on a Frozen Breeze

A snowflake just danced, with a spin and a roll,
While I tried to catch it, and fell on my bowl.
It giggled and sparkled, as I landed with style,
In a frosty embrace that made me recoil.

The stars start to wiggle with bright little grins,
As I join in their laughter, spinning 'round like twins.
Each flake tells a tale, with a funny little quirk,
Of snow forts and snowballs, and all kinds of jerk.

I ponder the chaos of winter's wild sway,
Where the snowmen conspire, and snowflakes play.
They whisper of mischief, of boots in the air,
While we tumble like acorns without any care.

So here in this wonder, my heart feels the freeze,
With dreams on the breeze, and a little unease.
But as I start giggling and fall with surprise,
Winter's a jester, under bright, twinkling skies!

Milton Keynes UK
Ingram Content Group UK Ltd.
UKHW021021251124
451242UK00021B/81